$\mathcal{G}$arden of Stars

Richard Mangulis

TO MY
FRIEND TIARA
MAY THESE WORDS
BRING YOU PEACE.
RICHARD
6-6-15

ISBN-13: 978-1502851345

ISBN-10: 1502851342

Photo of Blue Forest
by Andre Aleksis
andre@earthfoto.com

$\mathcal{P}$eace

in the heart

The best

joy of all,

more than gold,

and memories old,

and a newborn day,

and sun in the sky,

and the starry night-

is peace in the heart

from the heaven

above.

$\mathcal{B}$ lue Star

Blue star-
Who made you-
Who placed you
up in the sky ?
Wherever you are,
on what page of time,
and everywhere –
you showed the way,
when Christ was born,
to the wise men who came,
and spread His fame.
Philosophers spoke
and kings went to war,
and turned to dust,
but you're still there
and will remain,
your golden glow retain
and see us , be we near
or far.

ℬlue butterfly

Blue
butterfly-
when you fly
to the sun
in the sky,
will you slowly turn,
in the gentle breeze,
to return,
so not like Icarus,
you'd melt your wings
and burn.

$\mathcal{T}$he green

hills of home

Green
rolling hills ,
and air so pure
you can see
the far mountains blue,
and woodland deep ,
where creatures sleep
in soft beds
of moss and ferns .
The worldly cares
in the silence retreat ,
when God you meet ,
and hear the echo
of your heart.

11

$\mathcal{S}$*anctuary*

Ancient
mossy stones ,
and proud old trees
guard the gate
to a sacred place
where silence dwells,
and the world you can flee,
and safe be.

Who laid the stones
here long ago ,
and planted seeds
for the trees to grow
so fragrant and blue,
and the moss
in colors true.

In the silence
long strong roots
anchor our hearts,
like a gnarled old tree
from floods and storms
and all that may be.

13

♏usic

Heavenly
singing flows --
our spirit grows
with sweet sounds,
and memories,
and deep feelings--
music to the ears--
inspiration to the heart--
healing to the mind.
We rise
to greatness
above the cares
of the world.

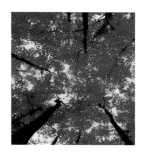

$\mathcal{M}$usic II

Angels sing
God's spirit flows –
our heart soars
to places known
and unknown ,
from the future
and the past ,
and things heard
and unheard ,
and seen
and inspired.
We rise
to greatness
above the cares
of our mind.

$\mathcal{B}$_lue_

golden night

Trees rise to the sky
to reach the stars,
and learn the secrets
they know,
from long ago
when the world was born
and mist rose
from the warm earth
to water the ground.
There were no clouds
and rain from heaven,
till after man was made
from dust-
and prophets spoke-
and Christ was born-
and armies marched
that are no more.
The stars that saw
the fall of Rome
still live in the night,
still shed their golden light
to warm our hearts.

$\mathcal{S}$*weet sounds*

in the twilight

Sweet sounds
in the twilight,
floating in the air,
like a song of prayer
of flutes
and harps and lutes
of angels,
playing the strings
of our heart,
to bring peace
from the noises
of the world
to the listening
eye and ear.

$\mathcal{V}$isions

Visions
of the night
leave with
the morning light .
Or do they in our
memory remain
to return
as deep feelings
of the past that last
because they were
so sweet.
Bitter feelings too--
could we not
just the happy
memories retain.

23

$\mathcal{S}$ ilence

In the silence ,
shadows deep,
earth creatures
dare not secrets keep
in the presence
of the hand
that made the waters
and the land.
Moisture rises
from the earth
to join the vapors ,
fog and mist
and rise above
the mountain tops
to join the clouds

Candles

Amber flames
ever glow
and upward flow
to rise above
the world below.
Great peace
into our hearts
they inspire
and give us joy
and light
and warmth,
and show a path
to our feet
so we can angels meet.

The mystery
in the sky

Beyond
the mountain range ,
a red blaze
of morning clouds ,
in the scarlet stormy
autumn sky,
hides the mystery
of the newborn day.
In the shadows deep
small creatures sleep
waiting for the sun
to unfold
and tell its secrets
to the world.
Be it storm or calm
not for us to know ,
or understand.
The beauty
of the moment
just to be enjoyed
by the eye.

29

Above
the stars

To dream,
to fly,
to walk
among the stars.
To soar
like eagles-
high in the sky-
where angels dwell.

Our science
and our measurements
define the borders
of our world.
But faith lets us
go beyond our
earthly instruments
and rise
among the stars.

We're on this earth,
not of this earth
and long for
our heavenly home-
where angels sing-
and glory
to our Father bring.

𝒯 orever...

Sun
sinks and rises
from the sea ,
paints mountain tops
in golden light
and travels
to the end of day,
and sinks again
into the night.

With two suns
we have been blessed,
one rises in the east,
the other sinks in the west.
And when the
red globe goes to rest,
a silver glow
in the starry night
lets us know
we're not alone.

Misty morning

Mountains

reaching to the sky ,

soft low clouds marching by

with a breath of gentle air

from a source unseen by eye,

ever closer to the sky.

Sunbeams breaking

through the mist

reach and touch

the trees and grass

to cleanse and nourish

newborn leaves.

A hidden hand

paints a secret land

with great green

forests far away.

35

$\mathcal{D}$ arkness falls

Darkness falls--
the night
our spirit restores ,
and calms our heart --
so we can hear
the voice of God
to show us the way
to everywhere .
The star,
that saw the land
where Christ was born,
still sees us ,
from afar.

S oft Heart

A spark--
to heal
to feel
to warm
the cold clay
of our heart
with inspiration ,
for a heart
that's like a stone
is alone
and does not weep
or love
or friendship keep .
May there be
a burning flame
to stir and feed
the seed
that's in us,
to grow and blossom
like an olive tree
and fruitful be.

39

$\mathcal{H}eal$

my soul

Why
does sadness last so long.
Heal my soul and
let me fly ,
to the sun in the sky,
like a butterfly.
And not dwell
on ancestral memories,
sadness and pain,
and peace regain
in the moments of joy
in every newborn day
to know and see
and fruitful be.

The old

stone gate

Secrets
and treasures
wait
beyond the
old stone gate .
Sit still --
Become invisible ,
and hear --
small forest creatures
drawing near --
the whispers
of the falling leaves --
the voices
of the plants and trees --
the fragrant alr
of evergreens --
and echoes
of the falling cones --
with green moss
growing on the stones --
all pleasures
to a needy heart.

43

The Sun

Rising
red glow
in the morning -
a promise or warning -
is a moment's joy
for us to know.
In the evening,
a golden bridge
across the sea -
as the sun smiles soft
upon your face.
The red globe sinks
in the ocean deep
- to rest -
then travel
to the lands of east .
The waters
and the winds
are help –mates
to push the waves
across the sea.
The sun
needs no helping hand--
it was granted a position
and orbit and station--
to smile upon each nation.

" When I lay me down to sleep,
I will not be afraid...my sleep shall
be sweet". Proverbs 3:24

𝓕*ear not*

Fear not-
be not afraid-
God will
His promises keep.
When you lay down
in peace, your sleep
shall be sweet,
and your soul
good memories seek,
from the past
and the future,
and places known
and unknown,
and heard ,
and unheard.
And the pain
of yesterday
will retreat,
will drain away,
to let you see
moments of joy
in the new day.

S _ilence_

In the silence ,

shadows deep,

earth creatures

dare not secrets keep

in the presence

of the hand

that made the waters

and the land.

Moisture rises

from the earth

to join the vapors ,

fog and mist

and rise above

the mountain tops

to join the clouds

$\mathcal{B}$e still
my heart

In the middle
of the night,
there came a knocking
at my door .
When I peeked out ,
to slay dragons
with all my might ,
there was no one there
to fight, or see
or fear or flee
--just anxiety--
great peace
came over me.

Made in the USA
Charleston, SC
06 November 2014